VOLCANOES
WHY DO THEY HAPPEN?

SPEEDY
PUBLISHING

Speedy Publishing LLC
40 E. Main St. #1156
Newark, DE 19711
www.speedypublishing.com

Copyright 2015

A volcano is a rupture on the crust of a planetary-mass object, such as Earth, that allows hot lava, volcanic ash, and gases to escape from a magma chamber below the surface.

Volcanoes are just a natural way that the Earth and other planets have of cooling off and releasing internal heat and pressure.

A volcano can be active, dormant or extinct state. An active volcano is one that erupts regularly. A dormant volcano is one that has not erupted for many years, although there is still some activity deep inside. an extinct volcano is one that has been dormant for over 2,000 years and has not shown any sign if activity.

Volcanoes are formed when magma from within the Earth's upper mantle works its way to the surface. At the surface, it erupts to form lava flows and ash deposits.

Over time as the volcano continues to erupt, it will get bigger and bigger.

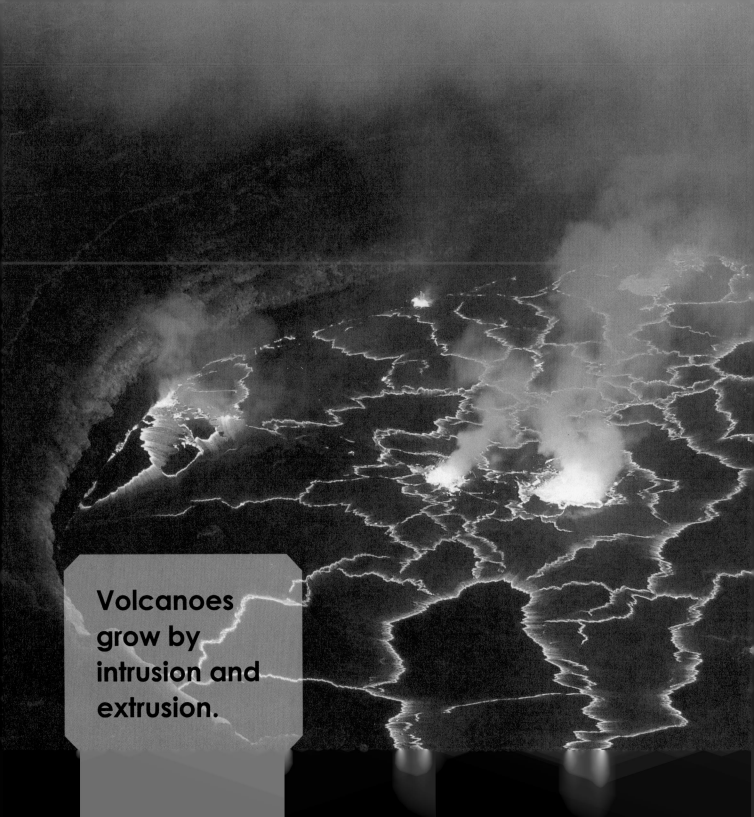

Volcanoes grow by intrusion and extrusion.

An intrusion is magma that moves up into a volcano without erupting.

An extrusion is an eruption of material that causes the volcano to grow on the outside.

Eruptions can occur without any preceding signals, making them extremely difficult to predict. Sometimes there are useful clues for judging when a volcano is likely to erupt. A volcano's history may provide some clues.

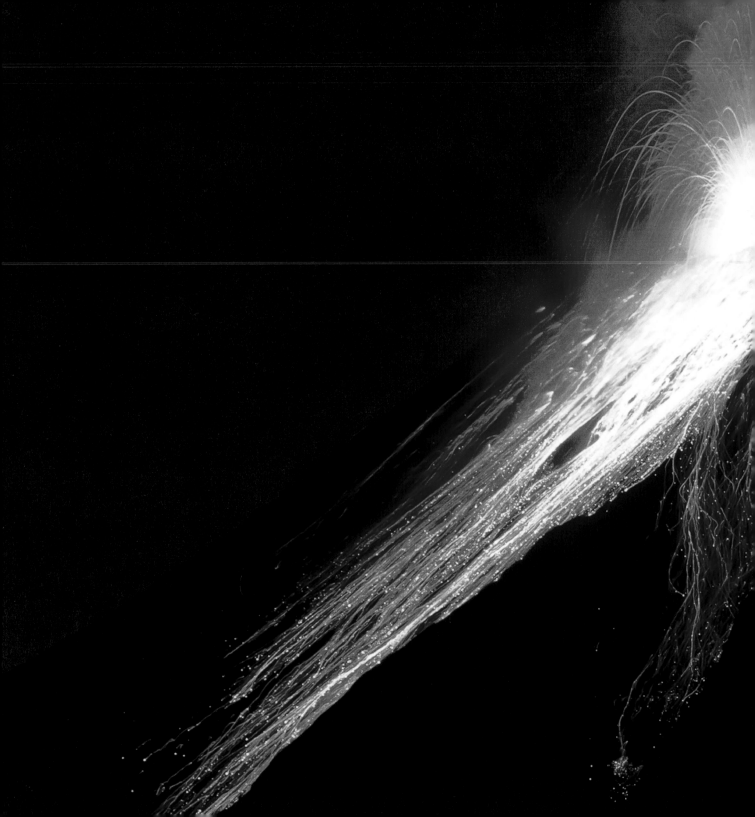

Volcanoes erupt because of the gas trapped inside magma, not the magma itself, ultimately forces an eruption. The types of gases include water vapor, carbon dioxide, sulfur dioxide, hydrogen sulfide, hydrogen chloride, and other very strong acids.

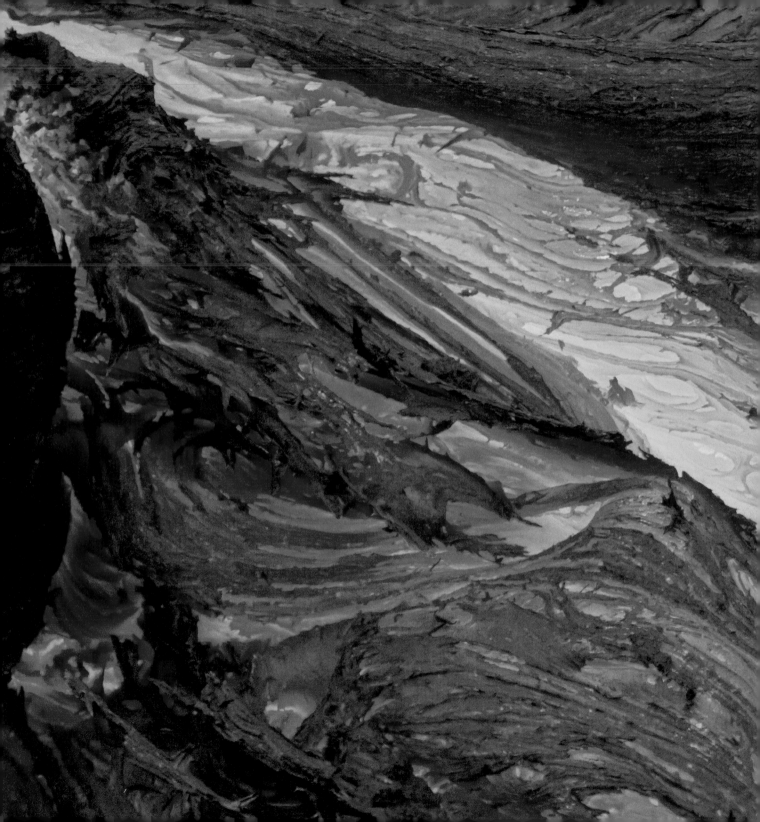

Magma deep in the mantle is under a lot of pressure, and so its gases stay dissolved in the liquid. It will rise to the surface or to a depth that is determined by the density of the magma and the weight of the rocks above it.

Bubbles start to form from the gas dissolved in the magma. The gas bubbles exert tremendous pressure. This pressure helps to bring the magma to the surface and forces it in the air, sometimes to great heights.

Magma reaching the surface of the earth is referred as lava. Over the period of time through constant eruption, layer by layer of lava builds up a volcano.

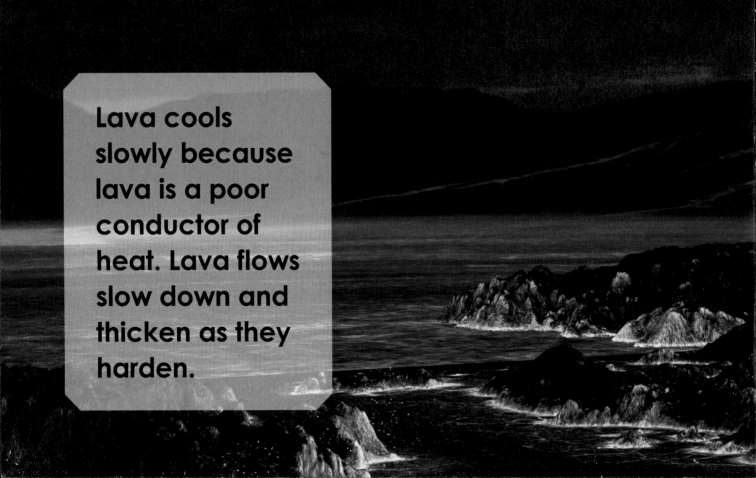

Lava cools slowly because lava is a poor conductor of heat. Lava flows slow down and thicken as they harden.

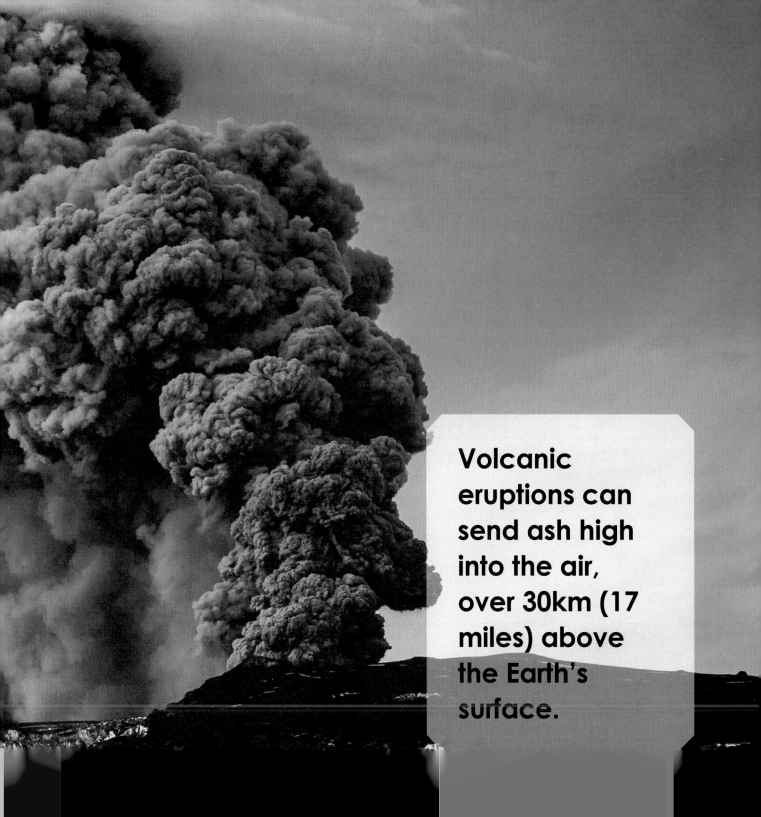

Volcanic eruptions can send ash high into the air, over 30km (17 miles) above the Earth's surface.